# Clown

Written by Jill Eggleton
Illustrated by Ann Skelly

Clown made
a shopping list.

# Shopping List

nose

hat

shirt

He went to the
nose shop.

He got a red nose,
and he put it in his bag.

He went
to the hat shop.

He got a yellow hat,
and he put it in his bag.

He went
to the shirt shop.

He got a purple shirt,
and he put it in his bag.

"Good," said Clown.
"I have a nose.
I have a hat.
And I have a shirt."

Clown went home.
He looked in his bag.
**No** nose!
**No** hat!
**No** shirt!

"This bag has
a big, big hole!"
said Clown.

Shopping List

nose
hat
shirt
bag

So...
Clown made
a shopping list.

And Clown went shopping!

# Labels

yellow hat

orange hair

red nose

purple shirt

pink bag

green sock

red sock

blue shoes

# Guide Notes

> **Title: Clown**
> **Stage:** Early (1) – Red
>
> **Genre:** Fiction
> **Approach:** Guided Reading
> **Processes:** Thinking Critically, Exploring Language, Processing Information
> **Written and Visual Focus:** Lists, Labels
> **Word Count:** 108

## THINKING CRITICALLY

(sample questions)
- What do you think this story could be about?
- What do you know about clowns?
- What do you think Clown could be writing?
- When would you make a list?
- Why do you think Clown wants a nose like this?
- What do you notice about Clown's bag?
- How do you think Clown feels about having nothing in his bag?
- How do you think Clown could have got the hole in his bag?
- Look at page 11. What do you think Clown could do?

## EXPLORING LANGUAGE

### Terminology
Title, cover, illustrations, author, illustrator

### Vocabulary
**Interest words:** clown, list
**High-frequency words:** got, it, have
**Positional word:** in

### Print Conventions
Capital letter for sentence beginnings and name (**C**lown), full stops, exclamation marks, quotation marks, commas